ERADICATING THE CANCER OF RELIGION

HINT: ALL PEOPLE HAVE IT!

DOMINIQUAE BIERMAN, PHD

ERADICATING THE CANCER OF RELIGION ©2009, 2020 by Dominiquae Bierman

All rights reserved. This book may not be copied or reprinted for commercial gain or profit. The use of short quotations or occasional page copying for personal or group study is permitted and encouraged. Permission will be granted upon request.

Unless otherwise identified, Scripture quotations are from the: NEW AMERICAN STANDARD BIBLE, Foundations Publications, Inc. Anaheim, California 92816 U.S.A. Used by permission. All rights reserved.

On occasion words such as Jesus, Christ, LORD, and God have been changed by the author, back to their original Hebrew renderings, Yeshua, Messiah, Yahveh and ELOHIM.

Bold emphasis or underlining within quotations is the author's own.

Published by Zion's Gospel Press | shalom@zionsgospel.com | www.zionsgospel.com
Printed in the United States

Paperback ISBN: 978-1-953502-06-3
E-Book ISBN: 978-1-953502-07-0

Kad-Esh MAP Ministries | www.kad-esh.org

52 Tuscan Way, Ste 202-412, St. Augustine, FL, 32092, USA | info@kad-esh.org

ERADICATING THE CANCER OF RELIGION

ZIONS GOSPEL
PRESS

DEDICATION & THANKSGIVING

This book is dedicated to all religious people world-wide and especially to those that do not believe in any religion and are their own religion.

I owe my very breath to the Creator of Life and to Him belongs all my thanksgiving. He eradicated the cancer of religion from my life, and in His mercy He has commissioned me to pass on the radical cure to you! HalleluYah!

CONTENTS

A Tree of Death. 1

Religion is Sin. 5

"Are We Blood Relatives?" 15

The Death of a Myth 23

Independence Day. 29

God is Love 35

Eradicating the Cancer of Unbelief 43

Your Ticket to Eternity = Faith 55

More Information. 63

Introduction

This book contains the most important *cure* of all: the cure from the cancer of religion! All people are religious in one way or another. Some are Christians, some are Orthodox Jews, Moslems, Hindu, Buddhists, New Age, Satanic Worshippers, Mormons, Jehovah's Witnesses, some Atheists, some Gnostics and some simply worship themselves! But we all worship something or other apart from an intimate personal relationship with the Creator. All religions (including "self-improvement" ones) will kill you sooner or later. It is time to eradicate the cancer of religion before it is too late!

My Definition of Religion

Religion is the human quest for knowledge, protection, provision, self-improvement and satisfaction outside of a personal, intimate relationship with the Creator.

This quest can be in the name of God, Judaism, Christianity, Islam, Buddhism and Hinduism or in one's own name or the name of Atheism, New Age or Gnosticism, or even the name of Satan. The common denominator is that it is all done apart from an intimate relationship with the Creator Himself. It seeks to know "about the Creator," "about the creation," but does not intimately *know* the Creator. In Hebrew, the root of the word "to know" is *yada*. This word is also used to describe the intimate relationship between a husband and a wife as they become one with each other. Then they know each other in every aspect. Religion of any kind seeks for knowledge *(yeda)* but does not know *(yada)* the One who is the Creator of *all*. King Solomon, the man that had more knowledge than anyone that has ever lived before him, said after seeking much knowledge, "because in much wisdom there is much grief, and increasing knowledge results in increasing pain" (Ecclesiastes 1:18).

Elohim, God the Creator, said in the Book of Genesis that man's quest for knowledge outside of Himself will kill us.

YHVH-Elohim commanded the man, saying, "From any tree of the garden you may eat freely; but from the tree of the knowledge of good and evil you shall not eat, for in the day that you eat from it you will surely die."

Genesis 2:16–17

We are living in an age where information and knowledge are available to all in abundance, but are we better off for it, or are we dying?

CHAPTER ONE

A Tree of Death

YHVH Elohim commanded the man, saying, "From any tree of the garden you may eat freely; but from the tree of the knowledge of good and evil you shall not eat, for in the day that you eat from it you will surely die."

Genesis 2:16–17

From the dawn of time, the Creator warned man against being religious. He warned them about the fruit of the tree of knowledge of good and evil. It was so serious that eating of it would cause death. A day in the Lord is like 1,000 years and thus, within the first 1,000 years of humankind on the earth, the first Adam died.

But do not let this one fact escape your notice, beloved, that with the Lord one day is like a thousand years, and a thousand years like one day.

2 Peter 3:8

However, another death happened instantly—a spiritual death. Adam, both male, and female, had enjoyed an unhindered and loving fellowship with the Creator of the Universe. After eating of the infamous tree, they got polluted and went from an open, transparent relationship with Him to a place of fear, guilt, and hiding. Their hearts and minds were not clean and pure anymore. They were polluted and intoxicated by the fruit of the tree of death, the Tree of Knowledge of Good and Evil!

When the woman saw that the tree was good for food, and that it was a delight to the eyes, and that the tree was desirable to make one wise, she took from its fruit and ate; and she gave also to her husband with her, and he ate. Then the eyes of both of them were opened, and they knew that they were naked; and they sewed fig leaves together and made themselves loin coverings.

Genesis 3:6–7

Why is it that desiring to know good and evil is so intoxicating and deathly? From the start, ELOHIM the Creator desired Adam (man and woman) to know Him only and to know everything else through Him—through His eyes—not in an independent fashion. Knowing anything *outside* of a personal relationship with God, figuring it out with our own reason and logic and not from a place of revelation, is *idolatry*. It is the attempt of mankind to be the god of themselves instead of having to rely on and answer to their loving Creator.

Idolatry is the foundation of every religious system, and idolatry is fueled by lust.

When the woman saw that the tree was good for food, and that it was a delight to the eyes, and that the tree was desirable to make one wise, she took from its fruit and ate; and she gave also to her husband with her, and he ate.

Genesis 3:6

Lust is an inordinate desire for that which is forbidden, sinful and harmful.

ELOHIM gave humankind the option of *knowing Him* or knowing the world without Him. They chose to be independent and to investigate knowledge on their own, and they fell from grace. This little quest cost them their relationship with the One that loved them, created them, and knew what was best for them. Every time that man ventures into a quest for knowledge for knowledge's sake or to obtain power, pleasure or satisfaction for his/her lust, they fall more and more apart from God. **All religions and cults, and of course the Occult and New Age, are based on a quest of knowledge to obtain power apart from God.** The only power that is holy is the one that comes from a personal, intimate relationship with ELOHIM Himself.

Adam had it all before the fall. They had an intimate relationship, the power, the intelligence, the unlimited wealth and riches, health, happiness and all the blessing which comes from living under the shadow of the Almighty. They traded all of that for *knowledge* and they lost the Knowledge of Him;

intimacy with the Father in heaven was lost. Sin came in; religion came in and the relationship was lost!

Adam could have eaten from all the other trees *freely*, but they chose the Tree of Knowledge and that tree killed them!

CHAPTER TWO

Religion is Sin

So He drove the man out; and at the east of the garden of Eden He stationed the cherubim and the flaming sword which turned every direction to guard the way to the tree of life.

Genesis 3:24

THE WORD "SIN" IN Hebrew is *chet*. *Chet* means "to miss," like, for example, when one is aiming at a target with a gun and one misses the target. When the woman and the man went on a quest for knowledge *outside of the boundaries of intimacy with the Creator,* they missed the target. The target was *knowing God.* From that intimate knowledge, they would have established an awesome human family that would have functioned in the Spirit of the Creator, in love, holiness, generosity and goodness. But instead of that, by seeking knowledge *outside* of His prescribed boundaries, they were polluted with sin and they bore a generation of religious hypocrites and murderers. That is the generation of Cain, the firstborn of Adam and Eve.

Cain did not cultivate a relationship of intimacy and obedience with the Creator, and yet he sacrificed to Him.

So it came about in the course of time that Cain brought an offering to the LORD of the fruit of the ground. Abel, on his part also brought of the firstlings of his flock and of their fat portions and the LORD had regard for Abel and for his offering; but for Cain and for his offering He had no regard. So Cain became very angry and his countenance fell.

Genesis 4:3–5

Cain got very angry that YHVH ELOHIM did not heed to his offering. ELOHIM tried to wake him up! "Cain, don't you see that you have cultivated the ground but not your relationship with Me!"

Then YHVH said to Cain, "Why are you angry? And why has your countenance fallen? "If you do well, will not your countenance be lifted up? And if you do not do well, sin is crouching at the door; and its desire is for you, but you must master it."

Genesis 4:6–7

The Creator was trying to instruct Cain, but he was too upset to listen! He wanted to worship the Creator with His head knowledge, with his reasoning, and not according to how the Creator designed and desired. He was religious, but He did not know God! That is the essence of every religious system:

Sacrifice without intimacy or obedience to the LORD of the Universe, YHVH-Elohim.

All religious systems influence us to seek knowledge apart from the Creator and His unfailing Word and Commandments.

That is why all these systems have external books that are more honored than the Holy Scriptures (the Bible) as given to the people of Israel. Even among the Jewish people, there are religious systems that have grown apart from intimacy with the Creator. These religious systems have various shapes and forms, but they are all called Judaism. Judaism is not based on the Torah and all the Canon of God's Scripture but rather on the Talmud and the Kabbala, which are external books that have replaced or interpreted to death the Holy Scriptures. These external books have gained a more prominent place than the *Tanakh* (Bible), and they are followed with fervor. Many religious Jews commune with the spirits of dead rabbis or other master guides apart from intimacy with the One and only loving Creator and His Word as given to Moses and the prophets that forged the nation. Judaism is based on sacrifice without obedience, and it is a sin of *idolatry*, it is missing the target altogether. The target is to *know YHVH personally* and not to "know of Him or about Him" from books that He has not authored and through spirits of darkness masking themselves as dead rabbis or other "ascended masters."

To know ELOHIM comes from the word *yada,* which is the same word that is used for "the intimate relationship between a husband and a wife in the matrimonial bed." From the beginning of time, ELOHIM sought to have an intimate relationship, like that of a husband and a wife, with His Creation—not in a sexual manner, of course, but I am talking about the closeness and the intimacy here that causes *oneness.* That is why He spoke through His prophet Jeremiah about a time when His people, the Jewish people and the people of Israel would know Him personally and not "about Him" or "of Him" from alien sources!

"Behold, days are coming," declares YHVH, "when I will make a new covenant with the house of Israel and with the house of Judah, They will not teach again, each man his neighbor and each man his brother, saying, 'Know the LORD,' for they will all know Me, from the least of them to the greatest of them," declares YHVH, "for I will forgive their iniquity, and their sin I will remember no more."

Jeremiah 31:31–34

We see through the Jewish prophet Jeremiah that YHVH, the LORD, promised that one day He was going to make a New Covenant with Judah and Israel. Through this New Covenant (Brit Chadasha), His people were going to get to *know Him (yada!)* personally and intimately! The forgiveness of sin that they would experience would remove the block that was obstructing this personal relationship.

Sin blocks and prevents a personal relationship with the Creator

When sin is removed, the relationship between humans and God is restored. The removal of sin for the House of Judah and the House of Israel would be through the blood of the New Covenant. Covenants between God and His people are always ratified by *blood*. We will relate to the issue of covenant by blood later on. For now, let us understand that the removal of *sin* from the Jewish nation and from Israel is through the blood the New Covenant. The removal or total forgiveness of *sin* would cause all of Israel to personally know the Almighty like Adam and Eve knew Him before the fall! This covenant was going to be different than the one they received on Mount Sinai when the Tablets of the Commandments were given,

"Not like the covenant which I made with their fathers in the day I took them by the hand to bring them out of the land of Egypt, My covenant which they broke, although I was a husband to them," declares the LORD.

Jeremiah 31:32

So, we are talking about another (blood) covenant that would happen later and would restore Israel to intimacy with the Father in heaven both as a nation and *individually*.

They will not teach again, each man his neighbor and each man his brother, saying, "Know the LORD," for they will all know Me, from the least of them to the greatest of them…

Jeremiah 31:34

As we know already, *to know* ELOHIM is to have a personal, direct, intimate relationship with Him both as a nation and individually! This relationship would only be possible through the (blood of the) New Covenant that would remove the stumbling block of *sin*. His people, now set free from *sin* and totally forgiven, would be able to develop (each one of them individually) a personal relationship with the Father in heaven.

The (blood of the) New Covenant would remove the sin of religion, which is the desire and the quest for knowledge apart from intimacy with the Creator. Through the blood of the New Covenant Israel would return (both individually and nationally) to oneness with YHVH, the loving Creator.

But this is the covenant which I will make with the house of Israel after those days," declares the LORD**, "I will put My law within them and on their heart I will write it; and I will be their God, and they shall be My people.**

Jeremiah 31:33

When the law of God is written in the heart, we do not break His Commandments to satisfy our lust for external knowledge and power. Adam (both man and woman) forsook the source of all wisdom to find it outside of Him and His Word. They believed the wisdom of the snake above the wisdom of ELOHIM. Every religious system seeks and believes the snake's wisdom above the wisdom of the Creator of the snake! They believe the wisdom that comes from created beings rather than the wisdom of the Creator. And the Creator in His wisdom said that eating of the Tree of Knowledge is *sin* and that sin will bring about death.

It has brought death to Adam and his family, to Israel and the Jewish people, to Christians, to Moslems, to Buddhists, to the Jehovah's Witnesses, to Mormons, to the New Agers, to Hindus, to Satanic Worshippers and all cults and occults.

All religious systems in the world are based on the *sin* of eating and studying from the Tree of Knowledge of Good and Evil, apart from the Creator's instructions. All the other sins, such as murder and immorality, come out of this one. Religion is the best hiding place for idolatry, immorality and murder. The knowledge of good and evil perverts the heart to the core and deceives people to "feel good about it," just like Cain felt good about His offering, and yet God rejected it. He rejected it because Cain was doing His own thing and not what He had prescribed. He was supposed to bring Him the First Fruits (like Abel did), but he brought him "an offering" (whatever he figured out). Apart from that, and even more serious, Cain's heart was not thirsty to *know* God. He was more interested in fulfilling his duty (sacrifice) without any personal relationship with Him. That is the reason why Cain's heart was polluted with hypocrisy, jealousy, rebellion and murder.

Then YHVH said to Cain, "Why are you angry? And why has your countenance fallen? "If you do well, will not your countenance be lifted up? And if you do not do well, sin is crouching at the door; and its desire is for you, but you must master it."

Genesis 4:6–7

Even after ELOHIM so lovingly spoke to him, he refused to listen. He loved his religion that made him "feel good," and his man-made religion made him a murderer.

Cain told Abel his brother. And it came about when they were in the field, that Cain rose up against Abel his brother and killed him.

Genesis 4:8

All wars in the world have happened because of *religion*

Then YHVH said to Cain, "Where is Abel your brother?" And he said, "I do not know. Am I my brother's keeper?" He said, "What have you done? The voice of your brother's blood is crying to Me from the ground."

Genesis 4:9–10

Religion makes people into hateful murderers! The fruit of *sin* is *religion*; the fruit of Adam's rebellion is Cain. Cain (religion) is the father of all religions, **and all religions are a vain attempt to serve God without God, apart from intimacy with Him.** Therefore, all religions will breed hypocrisy, jealousy, and *murder*. All religions and religious people are under a curse because all sinners are under the curse, and all people that do not know ELOHIM are religious in one way or another. The most prevalent religion today is the same one as in the Garden of Eden that caused the fall from intimacy and favor with ELOHIM: the religion of "self-improvement" through "more knowledge." This religion affects most of the sectors of the "enlightened" Western culture today. Most of the people in this New Age religious system blend very well with other religions and adopt a mixture of them into their belief system. However, we are talking about the same *idolatry* that caused Adam to lose the Garden of Eden: thirst and *lust* for knowledge apart from the Creator. Among these are various splinter religions such as "Atheism" and "Gnosticism." These are all religious systems based on *man* being the god of him/herself, and all of them lust for more knowledge to "improve themselves," be better people, more powerful, more influential, etc.

All of these mentioned above are under the same curse that Adam incurred for trying to get "knowledge" apart from ELOHIM. For wanting to know "secrets" but not to know Him, the only one who knows which secrets profit and which don't! The independence of man from His Creator has cost us dearly. Hatred, jealousy, murder, immorality and wars abound and we have lost our own soul! Once we pass on to eternity where are we going to spend it?

If you have not personally known the Creator on earth, you will not know Him in heaven. It is not about knowing the creation, or knowing about the Creator, but *knowing Him*, the One that created us, the LORD of the Universe—not "the universe"! Knowing any religious system (Christianity, Judaism, Islam or others) will not suffice. No amount of religious sacrifice or good works will do. These are all done "independently of Him" as an outcome of *knowledge* from the death tree of good and evil. People that are poisoned by that tree will do both *good* things and *evil* things. Whatever they "do," they are still outside of a personal, intimate (*yada*) relationship with the God that created them!

If you do not *know* (*yada*) Him intimately, you will spend *eternity* separated from Him, who is the source of all goodness and love. An eternity separated from Love, who is the true Creator, is an eternity in *hell,* just as Adam and Eve fell under the curse of their own rebellion and were cast out of the Garden of Eden.

So He drove the man out; and at the east of the garden of Eden He stationed the cherubim and the flaming sword which turned every direction to guard the way to the tree of life.

Genesis 3:24

Do you know Him? The key was handed to the people of Israel through the Prophet Jeremiah. He called it a *New Covenant*. ELOHIM-God is eager to restore us to a relationship with Him through the blood of the New Covenant.

"They will not teach again, each man his neighbor and each man his brother, saying, 'Know the LORD,' for they will all know Me, from the least of them to the greatest of

them," declares the LORD, "for I will forgive their iniquity, and their sin I will remember no more."

Jeremiah 31:34

The *sin* of idolatry, the *sin* of religion, will be forgiven through the blood of the New Covenant. But why "blood"? Isn't that cruel and disgusting? Can we not *know* God without the need for a "blood covenant"?

CHAPTER THREE

"Are We Blood Relatives?"

For the life of the flesh is in the blood, and I have given it to you on the altar to make atonement for your souls; for it is the blood by reason of the life that makes atonement.

Leviticus 17:11

WHEN WE MEET SOMEONE with the same family name, the question that arises is, "Are we blood relatives?" Do we belong to the same family? Do we carry the same genes, the same "blood"? The Word of God says that the *life* of the human being is in the *blood*. In other words, all that we are, the DNA of our entire being, is inside our blood. Genetics passes through the blood from generation to generation. Doctors are well aware of "genetic diseases," and in all medical questionnaires they ask about the illnesses that are most prevalent in the families. Psychiatrists are especially careful when handling patients whose family history shows depression or mental problems because of the tendency of those problems to reoccur in the next generations. Teachers are well aware that, for the most part, their students are an outcome of the genetics of their parents.

"The apple does not fall far from the tree," they say when they evaluate many of the students. The blood is the seat of our life! When a person bleeds, he is in danger of death; if he/she bleeds too much, they will die. There is no life without blood—our life is in the blood!

For the life of the flesh is in the blood, and I have given it to you on the altar to make atonement for your souls; for it is the blood by reason of the life that makes atonement.

Leviticus 17:11

Since the blood carries all the genetic code of our ancestors, then whatever they did or experienced affects us today. In fact, the Bible says that the sins of our fathers are visited upon us, the children!

You shall have no other gods before Me. You shall not make for yourself an idol, or any likeness of what is in heaven above or on the earth beneath or in the water under the earth." You shall not worship them or serve them; for I, the Lord your God, am a jealous God, visiting the iniquity of the fathers on the children, and on the third and the fourth generations of those who hate Me...

Deuteronomy 5:7–9

Elohim promised that whenever we break His Commandments by worshipping another god outside of Him, we and our next generations will be punished. The doctors and the teachers can recognize "good genetics" or "bad genetics"; they can see who is suffering from the sins of the ancestors in the realm of *idolatry*, having other gods besides the Creator.

We know that the sin of idolatry started in the Garden of Eden when Adam wanted to seek *knowledge* outside of His relationship with the Creator. **We have all inherited Adam's blood in one way or another.** We are all suffering from "bad genetics" in one way or another. Even those who are the healthiest and most successful in life are suffering from "bad genetics." At a certain point they will die from natural causes, disaster or disease, and once they do, they will go back to the dust and will be separated from the Creator for eternity! None of their good life on earth will help them then!

By the sweat of your face You will eat bread, till you return to the ground, because from it you were taken; for you are dust, and to dust you shall return.

Genesis 3:19

If the only predicament would be that we would sleep for eternity and "feel nothing," maybe that would not be so bad; however, this is not the case. We will sleep in the dust for a while, but then we will wake up to either an awesomely beautiful reality or the most horrendous predicament!

Many of those who sleep in the dust of the ground will awake, these to everlasting life, but the others to disgrace and everlasting contempt.

Daniel 12:2

How can we know whether we will be the blessed ones to enjoy everlasting life with our loving Creator or suffer disgrace and everlasting contempt away from the Creator, in a dark and painful place *forever* with no hopes of getting free? We can only know *if* we know what sort of *blood* runs in our veins. If the blood of Adam is in our veins, then we know that he sinned and fell under the curse because he chose the religion of knowledge instead of the *relationship* with the Creator. We know that he was cast out of the Garden of Eden and was banished away from the presence of God to disgrace and everlasting contempt. If we carry his blood, we will suffer the same predicament as Adam. But what am I saying? We all carry the blood of Adam, don't we? Or do we? Is there another option?

Blood for Blood

The blood of Adam was polluted with sin and religion, which would forever keep Adam and their descendants away from the presence of God. The bad genetics, the sinful DNA, would now be transferred through the blood from generation to generation. So, ELOHIM had totally lost *Adam* (male and female), the Crown of His Creation! Can you imagine the grief? They chose to go independent of Him to seek their own "knowledge"; they chose to worship however it seemed fit for them. What a broken relationship! And they were not even sorry or repentant; they rather chose to *hide* and covered themselves with excuses of *why* they did it!

Then the eyes of both of them were opened, and they knew that they were naked; and they sewed fig leaves together and made themselves loin coverings. They heard the sound of the LORD God walking in the garden in the cool of the day, and the man and his wife hid themselves from the presence of the LORD God among the trees of the garden. Then the LORD God called to the man, and said to him, "Where are you?" He said, "I heard the sound of You in the garden, and I was afraid because I was naked; so I hid myself."

Genesis 3:7-10

If they just *knew* Him, they would have repented and sought His forgiveness; but *no*, they did not know Him, so they hid from Him. All religion is the same: people hiding from the Creator behind "good intentions," trying to cover their sin and nakedness by man-made devices! ELOHIM is so merciful that He would have forgiven them and continued instructing them, but they chose to "take care of themselves" and to cover their nakedness with fig leaves. Of course, fig leaves can't cover, it is ridiculous! So, ELOHIM Himself had to cover them in spite of themselves! For the first time since Creation, blood was going to be spilt! An innocent animal was about to sacrifice its blood to cover sinful man.

YHVH-ELOHIM made garments of skin for Adam and his wife, and clothed them.

Genesis 3:21

Blood needed to be spilled in the garden to cover man's nakedness. Adam had lost the glory of ELOHIM, His presence that covered them. Now they would be covered by the sacrificial blood of an innocent animal.

For the life of the flesh is in the blood, and I have given it to you on the altar to make atonement for your souls; for it is the blood by reason of the life that makes atonement.

Leviticus 17:11

From the start, it was ELOHIM Himself who made the sacrifice for mankind. He is the one that covered man. The vain attempts of man to cover himself with fig leaves, good intentions, and religious acts are futile! The wages of sin is death—that is why an innocent animal had to die to cover sinful man. Man now would cause death to all creation; the spirit of death would affect man and beast the same. Man was to rule and care for the Creation, but the sin of man put the creation in bondage to sin. To get creation healed, we must get man healed from the deathly disease of the sin of rejecting the intimate knowledge of ELOHIM!

The only one that can cover and rescue us from the outcome of *sin* is Him, the Creator Himself! No religious system can replace Him! So, He sacrificed an animal to cover Adam. Later on, we will see that a whole sacrificial system of animals would be the only way for man to be forgiven and "covered" for one more year.

God called an idol worshipper to follow Him, to know Him, and to believe in Him. This idol worshipper was Abram. As Abram believed ELOHIM, ELOHIM made a blood covenant with Him and through Him with all His blood relatives, the children of Israel. It is to Israel that ELOHIM gave that sacrificial system to "cover" for sins.

And I will bless those who bless you, and the one who curses you I will curse and in you all the families of the earth will be blessed."

Genesis 12:3

Two Temples were built and destroyed carrying that sacrificial system that could never fully *free* man from the curse of sin, but only *cover* man for a while. But the root cause of the defiled blood was never dealt with. The root cause by which Adam lost "blood relationship" with the Creator was never healed. Adam still stayed independent from personal, intimate knowledge of ELOHIM until 2,000 years ago, when *blood* was exchanged for *blood*!

For the life of the flesh is in the blood, and I have given it to you on the altar to make atonement for your souls; for it is the blood by reason of the life that makes atonement.

Leviticus 17:11

It was ELOHIM who sacrificed the first animal to *cover* man, and ELOHIM Himself would have to give His blood to *rescue* man altogether, to *return* mankind to Himself!

"For the life of the flesh is in the blood, and I have given it to you"

"I have given *you* My blood to rescue you from yourself, your religion, and from your *sin*, to *save* you from eternal pain away from Me. You wanted to be independent, to seek for knowledge apart from Me, and your independence is costing you all eternity separated from Me. Not only in this life, but forever: you will be in darkness, in excruciating pain, banished from Love *forever*! After you die, there will be no more options; your fate in eternity is sealed here on earth! There will be no re-incarnations!"

Above all, the Creator is our Father. As a father He grieves for His children, especially for His Jewish children that He chose so that they can bring all mankind back to Him. He wanted His children back, like any good father or mother would and more so, since He is the Father of us all! So, He said, "I have given you My blood! I am willing to die that *you* may live!"

Can God die?

CHAPTER FOUR

The Death of a Myth

M Now the serpent was more crafty (arom) than any beast of the field which the LORD God had made. And he said to the woman, "Indeed, has God said, 'You shall not eat from any tree of the garden'?"

Genesis 3:1

MOST OF THE ANTI-SEMITIC crimes against the Jews have happened because of the belief in a dangerous *myth* that states, "The Jews killed God; therefore, the Jews deserve to die."

A few questions are provoked here: "Can God die?" "And if He can die, what would His blood do?" "If the blood of an animal in the Garden of Eden covered Adam and Eve, what would the blood of God do?" "Would we now have ELOHIM's skin, His own flesh to cover and rescue us—to redeem us?" "What does ELOHIM's skin look like?" "Does He have white skin, black skin, red skin, or yellow skin?"

Throughout the establishing of another deathly religious system called "Christianity," millions of Jews and others have been murdered. The Jews were killed because they were accused of "murdering God," meaning Jesus Christ, and others died for refusing to submit to their Christian religion. We have already established the fact that all religions bring about murder. Even among the most peace-loving Hindus you will find that religious clashes happen often, and they become murderers!

The Jews always murdered the prophets that ELOHIM sent to speak to them, to woo them back to Himself; the Christians have killed the Jews; Catholics have killed Protestant and Protestant killed Catholics; the Hindus kill the Christians and the Moslems; and the Moslems kill the Jews, the Christians, the Hindus, and everyone else that is not a Moslem!

Religion is sin and it brings death. Period.

Today in the sophisticated Western world people are not only killed physically, but they are also killed with words and attitudes. Hatred breeds hatred and religion always breeds hatred!

Death and life are in the power of the tongue, and those who love it will eat its fruit.

Proverbs 18:21

Those that practice the religion of New Age (worshipping the Universe rather than the Creator) or even the religion of *man* (man is its own god) or the religion of *knowledge* (knowledge is your god) are also murderers. They are establishing a life apart from the Creator and thus causing death to their children and their children's children. They themselves will go to an eternity without God, and they transfer this sin on to all their generations! It does not matter how nice your religion seems to be and how many hospitals and civic centers it builds (also

Freemasonry is a deathly religion, and it actually worships Lucifer or Satan), it all brings *death* – Eternal death!

So, what is the *myth* that we are dispelling here?

That anyone of us, be it Jew or non-Jew is able to bring about salvation to mankind. However, we can neither kill God nor bring life to man. We can do *nothing* to redeem humankind from its pitiful state of rebellion and separation from our loving Creator. No amount of human intelligence or knowledge will suffice! No amount of sacrifice or goodwill can change our corrupt blood genetics that we inherited from Adam. No medical doctor can do it. No amount of good intentions and good works will do! We are doomed to destruction unless we can have a *blood transfusion*. No amount of Jewish blood, royal blood, or whatever blood will do: All human blood is polluted with the sin of Adam. We must have another kind of blood, not from human source... *the blood of the Creator Himself!*

... I have given it to *you* on the altar...

Leviticus 17:11

Mankind cannot save itself! The very fact that we humans invent all kinds of systems and theories to save ourselves is proof enough that we are hopelessly *lost*. For trying to save ourselves apart from God or with a god of our own making is perpetrating the same sin of Adam, as they chose knowledge independently of the Creator and His absolute boundaries.

Elohim is a God of absolutes! His Laws are absolute. When He warned Man not to eat of the Tree of Knowledge, He said:

> ... for in the day that you eat from it you will surely die.
>
> **Genesis 2:17b**

There is more than one kind of death. There is physical death and there is spiritual death. Adam died spiritually; the *covering*, the glory, the presence of ELOHIM left him. He was naked just like the snake was naked. In Hebrew the word *arom* means both "naked" (no clothes) and "astute." The snake is described as *arom:*

Now the serpent was more crafty *(arom)* than any beast of the field which the LORD God had made. And he said to the woman, "Indeed, has God said, 'You shall not eat from any tree of the garden'?"

Genesis 3:1

The Hebrew word here is *arom*, which means "astute" or "crafty," and it also means "naked." Once they had listened to the crafty snake, naked of ELOHIM's presence and glory, they ate the poisonous fruit, and now they became *arom:* naked, astute, impure. They lost the *purity*; they lost God's covering of glory, and they became like the snake who was inhabited by Satan himself. They became like Satan!

He said, "I heard the sound of You in the garden, and I was afraid because I was naked *(arom)*; so I hid myself.

Genesis 3:10

The seeking of knowledge apart from the Creator and His Word will cause you to become *arom:* naked, astute, crafty and *impure*. That is the character of the snake that became imbedded in the character of humankind from then on... *Just check your thought life.* Even the best and most moral among us are impure; we are *arom*, naked, devoid of God's glory and presence, and we cannot save ourselves from this estrangement. Just like the fig leaves could not really cover Adam's nakedness, so our own devices cannot save us—none of them can! We are hopelessly separated from the Creator and cannot get back to Him on our own. The very belief that we are "good" apart from Him is *idolatry*. Again, we become the god of ourselves! The sin of idolatry is visited upon our children and children's children.

We cannot save ourselves; no amount of religion, philosophies, or theologies can make it. Our good intentions, sacrifices, good works, or kind acts cannot save us!

This is *the death of a myth:* Man is not all powerful! Man cannot kill God and He cannot bring life to himself—so, who can?

CHAPTER FIVE

Independence Day

I call heaven and earth to witness against you today, that I have set before you life and death, the blessing and the curse. So choose life in order that you may live, you and your descendants.

Deuteronomy 30:19

Now we can kill another myth: The myth is that we are *free* people and that *freedom* means we can do whatever we want. We are indeed *free*, but I'll tell you of what we are free from: We are free from the glory of God, free from the presence of God, free from his forgiveness and love. This kind of "freedom" is called *slavery*. We are enslaved to our own lusts and desires; we are enslaved to one another through perverted relationships of co-dependence and manipulation. We are enslaved to having or not having money, to our pursuit of career, fame, and self-fulfillment. We achieve one thing and then we are empty again and need to chase after another. Whether we do good or bad, we are enslaved to our emotions and passions. If things go well, we may be happy; if they don't, we get depressed.

We are enslaved to circumstances, trapped within our reality, whether good or bad. And eventually, this slavery will lead us to an eternity of condemnation and hell! Our independence from the Creator here will continue through eternity; our *freedom* is very costly! Adam's "freedom" cost them their relationship with God!

Now, they were free to do whatever they pleased and to pursue all knowledge they wanted, but they would suffer the consequences, and together with them all of us. God is a God of absolutes; His Laws will never change—He never changes! As much as the broken relationship with His children hurt Him, He cannot deny Himself. He is in integrity with Himself. As long as His kids want freedom from Him, freedom they will get. He gave them a free will to decide to be dependent on Him or independent of Him. They chose independence, which caused them now to become enslaved to the snake and to their own passions. The results are obvious all over the world!

His Laws are absolute!

However, God's absolute Laws will always be in effect, just like the Law of Gravity. *Ikaros* tried to defy it, and he died. If you jump from the 10th floor of a building, you will fall to the ground and most likely die. The Law of Gravity affects all of us, poor and rich, young and old, Jew or non-Jew, spiritual or unspiritual, good or bad. If we defy that law, we will die! Just like Adam that defied the one law. There are many more absolute Laws of the Creator. Take, for example, the law of sowing and reaping. It does not matter how rich, wise, kind, or moral you are in your own eyes. If you sow tomatoes, you will reap tomatoes. Whatever seed you put in the ground, that will be your reaping. No amount of money, intelligence, and goodwill can change that. God is a God of absolutes. He created everything after its kind!

The earth brought forth vegetation, plants yielding seed after their kind, and trees bearing fruit with seed in them, after their kind; and God saw that it was good.

Genesis 1:12

Men were created to be males, women were created to be females; tomatoes to be tomatoes, and cucumbers to be cucumbers. In fact, in nature when you try to mate animals of a different kind they cannot reproduce. Take, for example, a horse with a donkey that produces a mule, and the mule cannot reproduce. In other words, it causes *death*—the death of a kind! In the same way, homosexuality's fruit is barrenness and death, for homosexual couples and lesbian couples cannot bring forth children *by themselves*. The fruit of violating the loving Laws of the Creator is always barrenness, futility, and death!

Independence from Elohim's loving Laws brings death!

Yes, we are free to be independent of Him, but what does it cost us—and what's the solution?

The only solution to achieve true freedom is death to independence!

If independence from God's Laws and instructions brought Adam to such tragic results, so it gathers that dependence on Elohim and His loving instructions would bring about our healing. There is only one problem with this logical theory: *The bridge between us and God is broken.* Adam's sin, our ancestor's sin, and our own sin have separated us from God altogether. Our religious systems have granted us a placebo for a season, a pacifier, but we are totally separate from Him. **Just starting to do His Commandments and lots of good works will not mend the rift.** In the same manner that during The Holocaust, no matter how much work the Jews did in the concentration camps, they were not freed from the Nazis. At the entrance of Auschwitz, there is a sign that says: "Work makes you free." That was a deception—the more they worked, the more they suffered because they were in the hands of the cruelest tormentor, the devil personified in the Nazi Regime. They needed someone from *outside* to set them free from the concentration camps and death camps. Their work in the camps did not set them free, but the Allied Forces from outside managed to break in and free the prisoners. Someone outside of themselves needed to fight for them. They were helpless!

No amount of good works from our part can restore us back to the Living God! The moment that Adam rejected dependency upon the Creator, they put themselves into the hands of the cruelest tormentor, the devil personified in a naked, astute, *arom* snake. Satan now became the taskmaster, and any attempts of man to get free from him would become totally futile. Only one thing would work:

Faith: *Faith* in the goodness and the power of the Creator Himself; faith in His unquestionable ability and loving desire to free us.

Faith would be our ticket to independence from the snake and our restoration to an intimate relationship with the Creator; it's a faith that puts "all our eggs in one basket." We needed someone from outside of ourselves to set us *free*, and that someone is the loving Creator Himself! But would He do it? And if so, how? **We don't deserve it; we rebelled against Him—why would He do it?**

CHAPTER SIX

God is Love

But God demonstrates His own love toward us, in that while we were yet sinners, Messiah died for us... Greater love has no one than this, that one lay down his life for his friends.

Romans 5:8, John 15:13

ACTUALLY, I COULD END the chapter right at its beginning. There is just no more to add, but in this perverted and corrupt world, the very term 'love' needs to be re-defined.

A man whispers in the ears of a young lady, "I love you" with the sole purpose of having sex with her. A daughter whispers in the ears of a father, "I love you" with the sole intention of getting his money. A mother commits suicide, the ultimate act of betrayal, and leaves a letter of "I love you" to her son. People call pornography, adultery, and fornication "lovemaking."

So, when I state that *God is Love*, I do not mean that kind of perverted thing that comes out of selfish ambitions and corrupt motivations. I mean true love: selfless, unconditional, all-encompassing love. This kind of love is so rare nowadays, when one is willing to sacrifice his/her life for their loved one. In the famous movie, *The Titanic*, we can see an example of that kind of love when the hero puts his beloved on the piece of wood so that she does not freeze—while he stays in the water and freezes to death. He gives his life for her. She gets to live while he goes to his watery grave. That is a love that provokes much emotion. That kind of love can only come from God, the Creator of love.

As beautiful as the gesture of that young man in the movie was, it could only save one woman from a certain death, while all the others died. And it could only save her from physical death, but not from spiritual death for eternity. **The most selfless act of man, as amazingly touching, moving, and beautiful, is ultimately ineffective to save mankind both on this earth and forever!**

Then you will know that I, YHVH, am your Savior and your Redeemer, the Mighty One of Jacob.

Isaiah 60:16b

Only He can be the Savior of Israel and ultimately of all mankind. For ELOHIM chose Abraham and the people of Israel to be the carriers of the solution for sin and death. **Through Israel, salvation would come to all nations!** Forgiveness would flow like a river to all mankind!

However, when we read the New Testament, it says that God's love was manifested in sending His only begotten (not created!) Son.

For God so loved the world, that He gave His only begotten Son, that whoever believes in Him shall not perish, but have eternal life.

John 3:16

Remember that the Creator has made everything according to its kind? In the same way, He could only save us through His blood, through His kind.

I have given you the blood on the altar to atone (pay) for your sins.

Leviticus 17:11

Only He can pay; only He can free us—only His blood can set us free! According to medical science, a son always carries the blood of the father. So, we know that when ELOHIM gives us His Son to save us, His Son carries His blood! We know that this Son is not a mere human, but rather of the Godkind, as Isaiah the prophet tells us. This Son is also ELOHIM and in total unity with His Father.

For a child will be born to us, a son will be given to us; and the government will rest on His shoulders; and His name will be called Wonderful Counselor, Mighty God, Eternal Father, Prince of Peace.

Isaiah 9:6

This child will be born to Israel. He will be a Jew, and yet, as human as He will be, He is also divine. He is called Mighty God and Eternal Father. God Himself sends His divine Son to take the shape of a mere human, born of the tribe of Judah as a Jew in ancient Israel under Roman occupation. The blood of this Son will forever be the only sacrifice that will be needed for us to be forgiven and to be restored to ELOHIM.

I have given *you* the blood of my Son on the altar

The blood of the son is the blood of the father; that is a proven medical fact.

This child was born of a miraculous birth to a virgin, a lady that had not known a man. It had to be that way, so the Holy Blood of The Father will be in the Son. Only the Blood of the Father can save us, pay for our sins and restore us to an intimate relationship with Elohim.

Therefore the Lord Himself will give you a sign: Behold, a virgin will be with child and bear a son, and she will call His name Immanuel.

Isaiah 7:14

The virgin birth of this Son would be a sign to Israel that He is the Savior, the redeemer, and the rescuer – the Messiah! The name of this child is describing His position: Immanuel—"Elohim with *us*." In other words, Elohim has come down from His holy habitation to dwell here with *us*! Elohim came down as a man; the Son of God now became a Son of Man or another Adam.

Now the birth of Yeshua the Messiah (Jesus Christ) was as follows: when His mother Miriam (Mary) had been betrothed to Joseph, before they came together she was found to be with child by the Holy Spirit. And Joseph her husband, being a righteous man and not wanting to disgrace her, planned to send her away secretly. But when he had considered this, behold, an angel of the Lord appeared to him in a dream, saying, "Joseph, son of David, do not be afraid to take Mary as your wife; for the Child who has been conceived in her is of the Holy Spirit. "She will bear a Son; and you shall call His name YESHUA (meaning salvation) for He will save His people from their sins." Now all this took place to fulfill what was spoken by the LORD through the prophet: "BEHOLD, THE VIRGIN SHALL BE WITH CHILD AND SHALL BEAR A SON, AND THEY SHALL CALL HIS NAME IMMANUEL," which translated means, "GOD WITH US." And Joseph awoke from his sleep and did as the angel of the LORD commanded him, and took Mary as his wife, but kept her a virgin until she gave birth to a Son; and he called His name Yeshua.

Matthew 1:18–25

Yeshua means *salvation*

He was to save Israel and through Israel the whole world. He is born of the virgin birth; He is both a child and a Mighty God and Everlasting Father, and He was to be born in Bethlehem!

But as for you, Bethlehem Ephrathah, too little to be among the clans of Judah, from you One will go forth for Me to be ruler in Israel. His goings forth are from long ago, from the days of eternity.

Micah 5:2

An Eternal One, a divine One would come and would become Ruler in Israel. And He would come from Bethlehem!

Now after Yeshua (the true name of Jesus) was born in Bethlehem of Judea in the days of Herod the king, magi from the east arrived in Jerusalem, saying, "Where is He who has been born King of the Jews? For we saw His star in the east and have come to worship Him." When Herod the king heard this, he was troubled, and all Jerusalem with him. Gathering together all the chief priests and scribes of the people, he inquired of them where the Messiah was to be born. They said to him, "In Bethlehem of Judea; for this is what has been written by the prophet: 'And you, Bethlehem, land of Judah, are by no means least among the leaders of Judah; for out of you shall come forth a ruler who will shepherd my people Israel.'"

Matthew 2:1–6

So, the **love of God, His own Son,** was born in human form, in the form of a child of divine origin. He was born as a Jew and His name was Yeshua, which means "salvation." ELOHIM stooped so low as to become a man through His divine Son.

This Son now will carry a mission to term. The mission was to give the blood of ELOHIM Himself on the altar for the forgiveness of *sin*.

For the life of the flesh is in the blood, and I have given it to you on the altar to make atonement for your souls; for it is the blood by reason of the life that makes atonement.

Leviticus 17:11

The blood of Adam was polluted by *sin*, so no man could offer blood to rescue mankind; all human blood is polluted, and we are all children of Adam. Even if 1,000 people were to kill themselves "in the name of God," their blood could not pay, as it is polluted blood, which carries *sin* inside. Only the blood of God can do, and His blood was now inside of His Son that had no earthly father. The blood of His Father in heaven was flowing through His veins. Only that blood could reestablish the relationship between Mankind and the Creator.

But how would that holy blood be given on the altar? Murder? Suicide? Accident? How?

And after it is given, how are we to apply it? How are we to use it to cleanse us and to give us a blood transfusion so we won't carry the blood, the curse (and the separation from ELOHIM) of the first Adam anymore?

The only way to bridge the gap between the natural and the spiritual is *faith*. Faith working through love is the most powerful force in the universe!

For God so loved the world, that He gave His only begotten Son, that whoever believes in Him shall not perish, but have eternal life. For God did not send the Son into the world to judge the world, but that the world might be saved through Him. He who believes in Him is not judged; he who does not believe has been judged already, because he has not believed in the name of the only begotten Son of God.

John 3:16–18

Pray with me out loud, *"Father in heaven, Creator of the Universe: I believe; please help my unbelief! Reveal Your Son to me!"*

CHAPTER SEVEN

Eradicating the Cancer of Unbelief

And without faith it is impossible to please Him, for he who comes to God must believe that He is and that He is a rewarder of those who seek Him.

Hebrews 11:6

UNBELIEF KILLED ADAM'S RELATIONSHIP with ELOHIM. They disbelieved ELOHIM's Word to them and believed the snake instead.

The serpent said to the woman, "You surely will not die! For God knows that in the day you eat from it your eyes will be opened, and you will be like God, knowinggood and evil."

Genesis 3:4–5

When we disbelieve God and His Word, we are putting our trust in the snake, in Satan's lies. *He is a liar and a murderer.*

Whoever believes his lies and disbelieves ELOHIM's Words becomes a liar and a murderer just like him.

Yeshua spoke to the religious Jews of His time, and He says the same to all religious unbelievers of whatever religion and whatever nation,

> **You are of your father the devil, and you want to do the desires of your father. He was a murderer from the beginning, and does not stand in the truth because there is no truth in him. Whenever he speaks a lie, he speaks from his own nature, for he is a liar and the father of lies. But because I speak the truth, you do not believe Me.**
>
> **John 8:44–45**

The biggest lie is that God's Word is not true or not absolute. Satan's lies convince us to be independent of ELOHIM's presence and instructions. We believe his lies even when we think that Satan does not exist. **Our unbelief in something does not make it go away. I might not believe that *air* is a substance, for I cannot see it. Still, *air* will not disappear because of my unbelief.** You can think that God or Satan doesn't exist, but your unbelief will not change the reality that they do! In the same way, you can choose not to believe what is written in the Bible, but your unbelief will not change one word of it. It will all come to pass! So, unbelief only serves a purpose, and that purpose is to kill us! All religious systems work on the deathly foundation of disbelieving God and his Word.

Orthodox Judaism has replaced the Word of God for fables and myths of all kinds of sages and "wise men." They have forsaken the Torah and the whole Bible and have given themselves over to external books such as Kabbalah and Talmud.

There are many passages of Scripture that Orthodox Jews will not read because they obviously point to Yeshua, the Messiah, the Son of God and God the Son as the only way of salvation. The Orthodox Jews have been persecuting the Jewish believers in Yeshua for 2,000 years now! So, the outcome of this unbelief has been religion, and religion always breeds murder!

The religious Christians also have replaced the Word of God for interpretations of their liking through a deathly council called the Council of Nicaea. This Council held in the fourth century AD divorced all the Christians from the Hebrew foundations of faith, from the validity of the Torah and the Hebrew Scriptures, that was renamed "Old Testament." Through this Council a theology called replacement theology was established as church doctrine. This theology, like all religions do, has caused the murder of millions of Jews in the name of Jesus Christ, all the way to the Nazi Shoa (Holocaust).

The Moslems have not believed the Word of God, and instead, they believed another message carried by an angel that they said is Gabriel. Their disbelief of ELOHIM's Word and means of salvation has bred a murderous religion responsible for most terrorism in the world today.

I could go on and on, but I hope that by now you understand the principle: Disbelieving ELOHIM's Word brings about independence (rebellion) from ELOHIM and religion that causes murder. All people are religious, even those that say they are not. All men worship something or other. Some worship their money, some worship their art, others worship their "freedom" to disbelieve God and most worship themselves. They lead their lives as it seems fit in their own eyes, good or bad, completely independent of the Living God and the loving Creator!

Just like unbelief in God's absolute Law and plan brought spiritual and eventually also physical death in the Garden of Eden, so unbelief in ELOHIM's only and absolute plan for salvation means total death! We have already established that no man's blood can redeem, save, or rescue mankind and that no amount of good works can do it! Mankind, through Adam, fell into the hands of the cruelest tormentor, Satan, who will not let anyone go until they repent.

Repent in Hebrew means "to return"; it means to go back to what was intended from the beginning. The first thing we repent of is *unbelief*—unbelief that ELOHIM is a God of absolutes and that He is the Creator, separate from His creation. The obstruction between us is sin—the sin of unbelief that has made us knowledgeable of good and evil, and religious, wise in our own eyes, prideful. The only way to remove this death trap of sin is by receiving His blood sacrifice.

'For the life of the flesh is in the blood, and I have given it to you on the altar to make atonement for your souls; for it is the blood by reason of the life that makes atonement.'

Leviticus 17:11

He has given us the blood through His Son Yeshua. Yeshua lived, died on the Cross, and rose from the dead to please His Father. His blood is the blood of the New Covenant promised to the house of Israel and the house of Judah. It is the *Dam Habrit Hachadasha*, the "Blood of the New Covenant," through which we can be forgiven. Now we can turn from the Tree of Knowledge to the *true knowledge*, the intimate knowledge of ELOHIM through a personal relationship with Him.

"Behold, days are coming," declares the LORD, "when I will make a new covenant with the house of Israel and with the house of Judah, not like the covenant which I made with their fathers in the day I took them by the hand to bring them out of the land of Egypt, My covenant which they broke, although I was a husband to them," declares the LORD. "But this is the covenant which I will make with the house of Israel after those days," declares the LORD, "I will put My law within them and on their heart I will write it; and I will be their God, and they shall be My people. They will not teach again, each man his neighbor and each man his brother, saying, 'Know the LORD,' for they will all know Me, from the least of them to the greatest of them," declares the LORD, "for I will forgive their iniquity, and their sin I will remember no more."

Jeremiah 31:31-34

Outside of the New Covenant there is no forgiveness of *sin*, no salvation, and no hope to be reconciled with the Creator! He is a God of absolutes; there is no plan B or C, no manner of religion or of man-made devices, good or bad works that can save anyone. You can be the biggest philanthropist on earth, the best person that ever lived, the best Christian, the best Jew, Moslem, Hindu, Yogi, or whatever, but outside of the blood of ELOHIM's Son, Yeshua, there is no hope and no salvation. There is no other Covenant, only the New Covenant! The blood of the New Covenant is the only bridge to restore a personal relationship with ELOHIM from now and to eternity!

Unbelief can kill you for eternity!

Before Yeshua was crucified on the day of Passover, He said:

For I received from the LORD that which I also delivered to you, that the LORD Yeshua (Jesus) in the night in which He was betrayed took bread; and when He had given thanks, He broke it and said, "This is My body, which is for you; do this in remembrance of Me." In the same way He took the cup also after supper, saying, "This cup is the new covenant in My blood; do this, as often as you drink it, in remembrance of Me."

1 Corinthians 11:23–25

This awesome salvation was executed through the people of Israel. Yeshua was born a Jew after the flesh, though He carried the blood of ELOHIM, of the Father in heaven. He gave His life on the altar; He spilled His blood so that both Jew and Gentile could be saved and be restored to a personal relationship with the Creator. Through Him, we can become dependent on ELOHIM, instead of independent like Adam. Through this dependence on our Creator and through *intimacy*, He would write His absolute Laws and Commandments into our hearts.

"But this is the covenant which I will make with the house of Israel after those days," declares the LORD, "I will put My law within them and on their heart I will write it; and I will be their God, and they shall be My people."

Jeremiah 31:33

His absolute Laws and holy Commandments would now be written in our hearts and our minds. **Only *faith* can accomplish this, for faith takes us "from here to there."** Faith in Yeshua's blood sacrifice causes us to be reconciled with the Creator. And, once we are reconciled with the Creator through a relationship of loving intimacy—through His Holy Spirit, He teaches us His ways. He gives us revelation and the true interpretation of His Word.

In the name of His Son Yeshua, because He poured out His life unto death, because He took upon Himself all the punishment that we deserved, we have forgiveness of sin. The sin of unbelief and independence, the poison of the Tree of Knowledge is healed, forever!

The prophet Isaiah warned the people of Israel that such *great news* was going to be really hard to believe!

Who has believed our message? And to whom has the arm of the LORD been revealed? For He grew up before Him like a tender shoot, and like a root out of parched ground; He has no stately form or majesty that we should look upon Him, nor appearance that we should be attracted to Him. He was despised and forsaken of men, a man of sorrows and acquainted with grief; and like one from whom men hide their face He was despised, and we did not esteem Him. Surely our griefs He Himself bore, and our sorrows He carried; Yet we ourselves esteemed Him stricken, smitten of God, and afflicted. But He was pierced through for our transgressions, He was crushed for our iniquities; The chastening for our well-being fell upon Him, and by His scourging we are healed.

Isaiah 53:1–5

Since all men are religious by essence, one way or another, it is really hard for them to believe that someone has done all the work! It is hard to believe that the only thing we are required to *do* is *believe* and put our trust in what ELOHIM did for us. All religious systems are based on "what man can do." **The *only* plan of salvation of** ELOHIM **is based on what God did for us.**

Accepting and believing that will bring us to intimacy with Him. Whatever He will require that we *do* will come from a place of *intimacy* and *not religion!* His Laws and Commandments will all be written in our hearts as we commune with Him, His Holy Spirit, and His Word. They are the same absolute Commandments, but they are delivered into our being by His Spirit only!

Was Yeshua murdered as most of Christianity has believed? Millions of Jews have been persecuted and murdered to pay for the sin of murdering Jesus Christ. If He is God that came in the flesh, what kind of a God is He that can be murdered by mere men?

For this reason the Father loves Me, because I lay down My life so that I may take it again. No one has taken it away from Me, but I lay it down on My own initiative I have authority to lay it down, and I have authority to take it up again. This commandment I received from My Father.

John 10:17–18

No one could kill the Son of God; He had to lay His life down. This salvation has nothing to do with man's intervention. Elohim Himself, through Yeshua, accomplished it! He left His divinity to become a man, the Last Adam, to pay for the sins of the first Adam. And yet the blood that came out of His body was not normal human blood—it was the blood of His Father, Elohim, who, just as He promised, gave it to us on the altar.

> For the life of the flesh is in the blood, and I have given it to you on the altar to make atonement for your souls; for it is the blood by reason of the life that makes atonement.
>
> **Leviticus 17:11**

Until you believe in Him and in what He did for you, you are estranged from Elohim from now and all the way through eternity! That is called *hell* and hell is real. Whether you believe in it or not does not make it go away, but meanwhile *your unbelief is killing you!*

Only faith in the Creator and His Messiah, Savior, can save you now. Are you ready to believe and leave all religion behind? All men are religious. Religion is part of our human make up since we chose to be independent of Elohim. We worship the snake; we worship ourselves; we worship our freedom; we worship our good works, desires, money, other people, and other gods. All people are religious, and religion is based in *unbelief*—it is spiritual *cancer* that has been killing you without your knowledge. Are you willing to get healed? Or will you keep on taking "aspirin" for it? No amount of vitamins can cure this cancer. It is hopelessly incurable. The only cure is the blood of Yeshua, the blood that Elohim promised to the people of Israel. The same blood of the Father through the Son will heal both Jew and Gentile. Yeshua came as a man, but He was no mere man. He was God in human form. He carried the blood of His Father. No human blood could accomplish this salvation, as only Elohim's blood could. It is done, and now it is Your turn to say *yes* or *no* to Elohim through His divine and human Son Yeshua.

If you say yes: You live in intimacy and communion with the Creator here on earth and forever. He will give you His Holy Spirit that will guide you and teach you His ways. He will flood you with His love and empower you to live a holy and awesome life, now and for eternity.

If you say no: You die forever and spend eternity separated from God, who is love. You will spend eternity in a place much worse than Auschwitz, Majdanek, or Treblinka. Unbelief, independence, and religion will take you there. There is no hope of change after death, only judgment. That's it!

Your Judaism won't save you; your Christianity won't save you; the Universe won't save you; ignorance won't save you; your good works won't save you...

So it will be at the end of the age; the angels will come forth and take out the wicked from among the righteous, and will throw them into the furnace of fire; in that place there will be weeping and gnashing of teeth.

Matthew 13:49–50

But for the cowardly and unbelieving (even if they are "good people") and abominable and murderers and immoral persons and sorcerers and idolaters and all liars, their part will be in the lake that burns with fire and brimstone, which is the second death.

Revelation 21:8

Now at that time Michael, the great prince who stands guard over the sons of your people (Israel), will arise. And there will be a time of distress such as never occurred since there was a nation until that time; and at that time your people, everyone who is found written in the book, will be rescued. Many of those who sleep in the dust of the ground will awake, these to everlasting life, but the others to disgrace and everlasting contempt.

Daniel 12:1-2

He who believes in Him is not judged; he who does not believe has been judged already, because he has not believed in the name of the only begotten Son of God.

John 3:18

Can you afford *unbelief, independence* and *religion?*

Do you know that you will be alive tomorrow? Can you postpone a decision like this to "later?" Are you sure that this is not your last breath on earth?

Important: Believing in Yeshua as the *only* way of reconciliation with the Creator does not make you a "Christian." **It makes you a reconciled Child of God!** You do not enter into "Christianity" — you enter into the Kingdom of God. Yeshua was not a Christian; He is a Jew, and He did not come to give us "Judaism," but He came to call us back to the Father, to His Word (as given to Israel and the Jewish people) and to His Kingdom.

From that time Yeshua began to preach and say, "Repent, for the kingdom of heaven is at hand."

Matthew 4:17

The true faith in Messiah Yeshua, the Savior, is a Jewish faith, but it is not Judaism or Christianity. The New Covenant was entrusted to Israel and through the Jews salvation came to the

Gentiles. The true faith that saves will lead you far away from any religion that is man-made into an intimate *relationship* with the Living God and into total trust in His Word and Commandments, not the traditions of men! What was lost in the Garden of Eden was not a religion; it was *a relationship*. That is what the New Covenant in Yeshua's Blood comes to restore: relationship, intimacy, and communion with ELOHIM, and through it true life—from here to eternity!

That is Good News! ELOHIM will give you a new heart and a new spirit to worship Him and commune with Him. He will not remember your past sins anymore. This is a complete new beginning with no record of wrongs!

Moreover, I will give you a new heart and put a new spirit within you; and I will remove the heart of stone from your flesh and give you a heart of flesh. "I will put My Spirit within you and cause you to walk in My statutes, and you will be careful to observe My ordinances."

Ezekiel 36:26–27

Therefore if anyone is in Messiah (Yeshua), he is a new creature; the old things passed away; behold, new things have come. Now all these things are from God, who reconciled us to Himself through Messiah and gave us the ministry of reconciliation...

2 Corinthians 5:17–18

LAST CHAPTER IN THIS BOOK –
NEW CHAPTER IN YOUR LIFE!

Your Ticket to Eternity = Faith

> *Truly I say to you, unless you are converted and become like children, you will not enter the kingdom of heaven... And if My people who are called by My name humble themselves and pray and seek My face and turn from their wicked ways, then I will hear from heaven, will forgive their sin and will heal their land.*
>
> Matthew 18:3, 2 Chronicles 7:14

Do you find it hard to believe in such a "simple message"? Pray with me out loud to receive Yeshua. Father in heaven, I want to believe. Please help me help my unbelief! I ask Your forgiveness for my unbelief, for being independent of You, for worshipping and loving anything else above You, for seeking knowledge apart from intimacy with You, and for seeking pleasures by breaking Your Commandments. Please forgive me and remove my sins as You promised to do through the blood of the New Covenant. I choose to believe that Yeshua is Your Son, that He is all God and all man and that His sacrifice on the cross, His spilled blood paid the price for all my *sin* – that is Your blood that You gave for me on the altar. I accept and choose to believe in Him, and I ask You, Father, to give me a new life. Please give me a new heart and a new spirit. I pray in the name of Yeshua. Amen.

Yeshua, I say *yes* to You! Thank You for dying for me, thank You for saving me, and thank You that You did not remain in the grave, but You rose from the dead on the third day after Your burial – You are alive now and You will soon return to Jerusalem. Come into my heart and save me. I trust You from now on with all my life and reject all religious systems and all other religious beliefs. I trust only You to save me and to restore me to fellowship with the Father. I will pray in Your name, and I will walk and live in Your name. Please fill me with Your Holy Spirit so I can walk in love and power. Amen!

If you prayed this prayer by faith from your heart, you have now experienced a miracle! You have received a new heart and a new spirit; this is called a New birth.

Yeshua answered and said to him, "Truly, truly, I say to you, unless one is born again he cannot see the kingdom of God."

John 3:3

The Spirit of Elohim has now come to live inside of you, and He wants to fill you completely with his presence and power. **If you are willing to follow Yeshua all the way and to get rid of all that offends the living God, say, "YES!"**

If you said "Yes!" pray with me now for the baptism in the Holy Spirit.

And they were all filled with the Holy Spirit and began to speak with other tongues, as the Spirit was giving them utterance.

Acts 2:4

Beloved heavenly Father, please fill me with Your Holy Spirit and Holy Fire all the way. I completely surrender to You. In Yeshua's name I pray.

Lift your hands to Him and worship Him. Let Him touch you and fill you. He is *real!* You may feel the urge to speak some words with your mouth, and it may be that you have never spoken these words before. This is called "praying in tongues," which is a sign that you have been filled with the Holy Spirit. Remember that the presence of ELOHIM is new to you, and so are the sensations; just keep on praising Him and thanking Him like a little child and abandon yourself to His presence. His presence was lost in the garden due to sin; now His presence will wash you clean.

If nothing happened, ask Him to reveal to you what is obstructing you, and do what He says. He is eager to talk to you; you are His lamb now and His sheep hear His voice!

Yeshua said,

My sheep hear My voice, and I know them, and they follow Me;

John 10:27

Commune with ELOHIM through Yeshua; He has died to restore you to intimacy with Him. Remember that *sin* broke the relationship, so get rid of all known sin and ask Him to show you what is sin in His eyes.

Read, Meditate, Proclaim and Do His Word

The Bible from Genesis to Revelation (both covenants) is the Word of ELOHIM. Start to read the Bible from the beginning and read it all, again, and again, and again. Pray that His Holy Spirit will reveal His Word to you. You can never get too much revelation; He always has more! In most Bible translations, Yeshua will be called Jesus, but that is not His real birth name—His true name is Yeshua. Try to get a Bible that is translated directly from the Hebrew. Believe what you read, and *do* what He says to do. His Holy Spirit will guide you.

This book of the law shall not depart from your mouth, but you shall meditate on it day and night, so that you may be careful to do according to all that is written in it; for then you will make your way prosperous, and then you will have success.

Joshua 1:8

Fellowship with other believers

ELOHIM has made Jews and Gentiles in the Messiah into *one* people: *One New Man*. Yet, because men tend to be religious, there are many denominations and groups that claim to have the absolute truth. Most of them believe that Christianity is the way and they have forgotten that Yeshua, the Jewish Messiah is the Way. Pray for *Abba* (Father) to lead you to the believers that He wants you to meet. Write to us and request our advice on this; we may have a group of true believers in your area.

For where two or three have gathered together in My name, I am there in their midst.

> Matthew 18:20

Be baptized by full immersion into the name of Yeshua

He who has believed and has been baptized shall be saved; but he who has disbelieved shall be condemned.

> Mark 16:16

In Hebrew this is called a "mikveh." All Jewish brides must go through the mikveh (be immersed) before their wedding. Now we have "married" Yeshua and we need to be baptized in identification with Him and to remove all sin. This is to be done preferably inside of a body of living water like a river, a lake or the sea. If none is available, a swimming pool or water tank will do.

You need to be baptized (by *full* immersion) **into the name of Yeshua**. This is like a betrothal ceremony. He is giving you His name; He is now your promised husband. You are to worship no other gods. (Whether we are men or women, we commit to Yeshua in the same manner that a wife commits to a husband. Remember that He is ELOHIM, neither male nor female, and at the same time He has the attributes of both male and female.)

This act of faith shows that you mean business with Him and that you have genuinely repented of your former independence of Him.

Go and tell others about Yeshua

Go therefore and make disciples of all the nations, baptizing them – teaching them to observe all that I commanded you; and lo, I am with you always, even to the end of the age.

Matthew 28:19-20

Remember that all the other people that you know are, for the most part, *lost* and do not know Yeshua. They are still in sin, unbelief, independence, and religion. You cannot force them to believe, but you can tell them the truth and share what happened to you. You can also give them this book to read and pray for them, asking the Father to open their hearts to the Truth.

Greater Works

When Yeshua walked this earth in Israel, He did amazing miracles! Everyone that came to Him was healed. You too as a believer can do the same miracles in His name,

Truly, truly, I say to you, he who believes in Me, the works that I do, he will do also; and greater works than these he will do; because I go to the Father. Whatever you ask in My name, that will I do, so that the Father may be glorified in the Son. If you ask Me anything in My name, I will do it.

John 14:12-14

These signs will accompany those who have believed: in My name they will cast out demons, they will speak with new tongues; they will pick up serpents, and if they drink any deadly poison, it will not hurt them; they will lay hands on the sick, and they will recover.

Mark 16:17–18

Deliverance

All of us that come to Yeshua need deliverance. We have all been away from the Father in heaven and, without our knowledge or with our full knowledge, we have been involved with evil spirits. Even seemingly innocent things like reading the horoscope, yoga, meditation, harboring hatred, or having sex outside of marriage with men or women can do that. All sin (which we all have!) opens us up to the demonic realm. Some of us have come from "cleaner" backgrounds and yet we still need deliverance. You can ask the Father to lead you to a wholesome congregation of believers where you may receive deliverance. Ask Him, and He will give it to you!

If you ask Me anything in My name, I will do it.

John 14:14

Pray for Israel and Love Israel

Pray for the peace of Jerusalem: "May they prosper who love you."

Psalms 122:6

If you are a Jew, you probably have to rediscover your roots and ELOHIM's Word, the Tanakh, and the Brit Chadasha, the Bible.

If you are a Gentile or an Arab, you need to rediscover Israel. There is no New Covenant without Israel and no salvation without the Jews. God chose Yeshua to be born Jewish. For more on this very important subject, go to our website www.kad-esh.org and order my books *The Healing Power of the Roots*, *Sheep Nations* and *Grafted In*.

For our GRM Bible School, go to www.grmbibleschool.com
Tell us how this book has impacted your life. Write to:

info@kad-esh.org or to:
52 Tuscan Way, Ste. 202-412
St. Augustine, FL. 32092 USA
Phone: +1 (972) 301-7087

Welcome to your new life, free from the cancer of religion! *Welcome to the New Covenant!*

They will not teach again, each man his neighbor and each man his brother, saying, 'Know YHVH,' for they will all know Me, from the least of them to the greatest of them," declares YHVH, "for I will forgive their iniquity, and their sin I will remember no more."

Jeremiah 31:34

We love you and care for you!

APPENDIX

More Information

Other Books by Archbishop Dominiquae Bierman

Order now online: www.kad-esh.org/shop/

The Identity Theft
The Return of the 1st Century Messiah

Restoring the Glory – Volume I: The Original Way
The Ancient Paths Rediscovered

The MAP Revolution (Free E-Book)
Find Out Why Revival Does Not Come... Yet!

The Healing Power of the Roots
It's a Matter of Life or Death!

Grafted In
The Return to Greatness

Sheep Nations
It's Time to Take the Nations!

Stormy Weather
Judgment Has Already Begun, Revival is Knocking at the Door

Yeshua is the Name
The Important Restoration of the Original Hebrew Name of the Messiah

The Bible Cure for Africa and the Nations
The Key to the Restoration of All Africa

The Key of Abraham
The Blessing... or the Curse?

Yes!
Archbishop Dominiquae Bierman's Dramatic Testimony of Salvation

Restoration of Holy Giving
Releasing the True 1,000-Fold Blessing

Vision Negev
The Awesome Restoration of the Sephardic Jews

Defeating Depression
This Book is a Kiss from Heaven

From Sickology to a Healthy Logic
The Product of 18 Years Walking Through Psychiatric Hospitals

ATG: Addicts Turning to God
The biblical Way to Handle Addicts and Addictions

The Woman Factor by Rabbi Baruch Bierman
Freedom From Womanophobia

The Spider That Survived Hurricane Irma
God's Call for America to Repent

The Revival of the Third Day (Free E-Book)
The Return to Yeshua the Jewish Messiah

Also Available

Music Albums
www.kad-esh.org/shop/
The Key of Abraham
Abba Shebashamayim
Uru
Retorno

Get Equipped & Partner With Us

Global Revival MAP (GRM) Israeli Bible School
Take the most comprehensive video Bible school online that focuses on dismantling replacement theology. For more information or to order, please contact us:
www.grmbibleschool.com
grm@dominiquaebierman.com

United Nations for Israel Movement
We invite you to join us as a member and partner with $25 a month, which supports the advancing of this End time vision that will bring true unity to the body of the Messiah. We will see the One New Man form, witness the restoration of Israel, and take part in the birthing of Sheep Nations. Today is an exciting time to be serving Him!
www.unitednationsforisrael.org
info@unitednationsforisrael.org

Global Re-Education Initiative Against Anti-Semitism (GRI)
Discover the Jewishness of Jesus and defeat Religious anti-Semitism with this online course to see revival in your nation!
www.against-antisemitism.com
info@against-antisemitism.com

Join Our Annual Israel Tours
Travel through the Holy Land and watch the Hebrew Holy Scriptures come alive.
www.kad-esh.org/tours-and-events/

To Send Offerings to Support our Work
Your help keeps this mission of restoration going far and wide.
www.kad-esh.org/donations

CONTACT US

Archbishop Dr. Dominiquae & Rabbi Baruch Bierman
Kad-Esh MAP Ministries | www.kad-esh.org | info@kad-esh.org
United Nations for Israel | www.unitednationsforisrael.org
info@unitednationsforisrael.org
Zion's Gospel Press | shalom@zionsgospel.com
52 Tuscan Way, Ste 202-412, 32092 St. Augustine Florida, USA
+1-972-301-7087

www.ingramcontent.com/pod-product-compliance
Lightning Source LLC
Chambersburg PA
CBHW021431070526
44577CB00001B/155